ALBERT EINSTEIN

Published by Creative Education
123 South Broad Street
Mankato, Minnesota 56001
Creative Education is an imprint of The Creative Company.

DESIGN AND PRODUCTION **EVANSDAY DESIGN**

PHOTOGRAPHS BY Corbis (Lucien Aigner, Austrian Archives, Bettmann,
CORBIS SYGMA, Aaron Horowitz, Don Mason, Leonard de Selva),
The Granger Collection, New York

Excerpt from THE WORLD AS I SEE IT reprinted by permission of
Citadel Press / Kensington Publishing Corp. www.kensingtonbooks.com

LIBRARY OF CONGRESS CATALOGING-IN-PUBLICATION DATA
Frisch, Aaron.
Albert Einstein / by Aaron Frisch.
p. cm. – (Genius)
Summary: A biography of the twentieth-century physicist whose theories
of relativity revolutionized the way we look at space and time.
ISBN 1-58341-328-6
1. Einstein, Albert, 1879–1955—Juvenile literature. 2. Physicists—Biography—Juvenile literature.
[1. Einstein, Albert, 1879–1955. 2. Physicists. 3. Scientists. 4. Nobel Prizes—Biography.]
I. Title. II. Genius (Mankato, Minn.)

QC16.E5.F78 2004
530'.092—dc22   2003065227

First edition

9 8 7 6 5 4 3 2 1

GENiUS

MERIDIAN MIDDLE SCHOOL
2195 Brandywyn Lane
Buffalo Grove IL 6008

Aaron Frisch

HIS NAME IS SYNONYMOUS WITH GENIUS.
IT HAS BEEN SO SINCE THE EARLY 20TH CENTURY, WHEN AS AN
EAGER YOUNG SCIENTIST WITH SLEEPY-LOOKING EYES, HE MADE
ORDER OF THE UNIVERSE AS WE KNOW IT. BUT OUR FASCINA-
TION WITH HIM IS ABOUT MUCH MORE THAN SCIENCE. IT IS
ABOUT A MAN OF CONTRADICTIONS. A GENIUS WITH A NOTO-
RIOUSLY POOR MEMORY. A LOVER OF HUMANKIND WHO WAS A
SELF-PROCLAIMED "LONE TRAVELER." A PACIFIST WHO ADVO-
CATED THE CREATION OF THE ATOMIC BOMB. A NONRELIGIOUS
MAN WHO WAS A CHAMPION OF JEWISH CAUSES. A FIGURE LOVED
BY THE WORLD BUT DISTRUSTED BY GOVERNMENTS. ALL OF THESE
THINGS AND MORE MAKE UP THE LEGACY OF ALBERT EINSTEIN.

GENIUS

1 A EUROPEAN UPBRINGING

ALBERT EINSTEIN'S BIRTH, ON MARCH 14, 1879, IN THE GERMAN TOWN OF ULM, CAUSED A STIR. HIS HEAD WAS SO LARGE AND ODDLY SHAPED THAT HIS MOTHER, PAULINE, AT FIRST FEARED SHE HAD GIVEN BIRTH TO A DEFORMED CHILD. ALTHOUGH THE STRIKING APPEARANCE FADED OVER TIME, ALBERT'S HEAD WOULD REMAIN LARGER THAN NORMAL THROUGHOUT HIS LIFE.

A compass piqued young Einstein's curiosity

When Albert was a year old, the Einsteins moved to the city of Munich, where his father, Hermann, and uncle Jakob ran a small electrical engineering business. There Pauline continued to fret over her young son, who turned three before speaking and then spoke only haltingly for several years. Young Albert loved building blocks and would spend hours erecting tall towers with playing cards. He preferred to play by himself, and his closest childhood friend was his little sister, Maja, who was born in 1881.

As a child, Albert's quiet nature and droopy eyelids created the impression that he was interested in nothing. In fact, he was interested in everything. One day Hermann showed his five-year-old son a compass. Albert was fascinated by the fact that the red needle always pointed in the same direction. "I can still remember . . . that this experiment made a deep and lasting impression upon me," he later wrote. "Something deeply hidden had to be behind things."

When he was six, Albert began attending a local Catholic elementary school. The Einsteins were Jewish, but they did not actively practice their faith and chose the school for its educational quality rather than its religious affiliation. Albert hated school. The students were made to wear uniforms, and he resisted the rigidity of the instruction and the fact that success hinged mainly on memorization. Refusing to unthinkingly accept everything his teachers said, he received mediocre grades.

In many respects, Albert's schooling began when he went home. His mother taught him to play the violin, and Albert frequently played algebra games with his father and uncle, who both possessed sharp mathematical minds. He also came in contact with Max Talmud, a college student and family friend who introduced Albert to books on algebra, science, and philosophy. As he approached his teens, Albert peppered his household elders with questions on such topics as light and movement. At the age of 12, Albert astonished his father and uncle by producing an original proof for the Pythagorean theorem.

In 1894, as Albert began his high school education at Munich's Luitpold Gymnasium, failing business prompted the Einstein family to move to a town near Milan, Italy. Albert stayed behind to finish school, which he soon found unbearable. Luitpold Gymnasium was terribly strict, and it stressed the arts and humanities while almost completely ignoring the latest developments in science. Albert's disinterest and obvious intelligence irritated his instructors so much that one day his teacher

"He was even considered backward by his teachers. He told me that he was mentally slow, unsociable, and adrift forever in his foolish dreams."

HANS ALBERT EINSTEIN
ALBERT'S ELDER SON

In his youth, Einstein was a mediocre student with the tendencies of a dreamer; in this photograph, he poses (right) at age eight with his sister, Maja.

suggested he leave, snapping, "You sit in the back row and smile, and that violates the feeling of respect which a teacher needs from his class."

Albert took this advice and joined his family in Italy. Hermann then tried to place him at Zurich Polytechnic (later known as the Federal Institute of Technology), a renowned scientific college in Switzerland. Albert took the entrance exam and failed; he aced the physics and math sections but failed the language and history portions. After spending a year at a Swiss high school, 17-year-old Albert was finally admitted to Zurich Polytechnic, where he studied in hopes of becoming a science teacher.

In college, too, Albert found much of the instruction boring and frequently skipped classes so he could indulge in scientific and mathematical materials of his choosing. Whenever an exam came up, he would borrow the notes of his friend Marcel Grossman, cram, pass the test, and then return to his own pursuits. His professors recognized his potential, but most of them found his work ethic deplorable, with one going so far as to call him a "lazy dog."

One of the students Albert spent time with during these years was Mileva Maric, the only woman in his class. They soon fell in love, and in 1902, Mileva would give birth to a girl named Lieserl. It is not known what became of the couple's baby, although it is likely she was given up for adoption.

EINSTEIN TAKES A JOB AS A TECHNICAL EXAMINER AT THE PATENT OFFICE IN BERN, SWITZERLAND. *Timeline* 1902

Einstein liked to joke around in school, but when called upon to prove his mathematical genius, he rose to the challenge, taking human knowledge to new heights.

2 THE YEAR OF MIRACLES

English scientist Isaac Newton

As a patent examiner, Albert reviewed proposals for new inventions and described any faults. The job seemed a lowly one for such a gifted young man, but Albert loved it, later calling these years the best of his life.

Having secured a reasonably well-paying job, Albert married Mileva in 1903. In 1904, they had a son named Hans Albert; they would have a second son, named Edward, six years later. Albert now divided his time three ways: among his growing family, his job, and independent exploration of several physics ideas, or theories, he had developed. Of the three, he threw himself most furiously into his theories. Much of his work consisted simply of deep reflection, as he had the incredible ability to envision answers to his questions through mere thought.

It was an exciting time to be a scientist. The field of physics had long revolved around ideas, or "laws," set forth in the 1660s by English scientist Isaac Newton, but scientists were now finding more and more things Newton's laws could not explain. In his solitary hours of thought, Albert came to reject some of Newton's ideas—such as the notion that the universe was filled with a mysterious substance called ether—and offer his own answers to the mysteries of the "huge world."

In 1905, at the age of 26, Albert published several earth-shaking proposals in the German journal *Annalen der Physik* (*Annals of Physics*). The world's greatest physicists were stunned. Who, they wondered, was this young unknown—isolated from the scientific community and unable to attain even the lowliest academic position—who dared challenge Newton?

One of the most amazing things about Albert's 1905 papers was the broad spectrum they covered. One paper proposed a means of using tiny particles suspended in liquid to prove the existence of atoms. Another built on the previous work of German physicist Max Planck and explained that when light hits certain kinds of metal, atomic particles are released and electricity is produced—a phenomenon known as the photoelectric effect. This discovery would eventually lead to such inventions as television, automatic streetlights, and lasers.

A third—and most significant—paper explained Albert's special theory of relativity. This fantastically complex theory basically stated that space and time are not un-changing, as Newton believed. Instead, they are relative, or change depending on whether the observer is moving or at rest. The theory considered time a fourth di-mension (adding it to length, width, and height) and explained Albert's belief that

This photo shows Einstein conversing with Max Planck at a scientific conference in Berlin; the two renowned physicists built upon each other's work.

Timeline **1905** IN HIS "YEAR OF MIRACLES," EINSTEIN PUBLISHES SEVERAL REVOLUTIONARY PHYSICS THEORIES.

16

all objects with mass, when moving at extremely high speeds through "space-time," are compressed and experience a slowing of time, making such science-fiction concepts as time travel a reality. From this theory came the formula $E=mc^2$, which stated that a tiny amount of mass could be turned into a tremendous amount of energy if made to move fast enough.

The 1905 papers were, as French physicist Louis de Broglie said, "blazing rockets which in the dark of the night suddenly cast a brief but powerful illumination over an immense unknown region." The year 1905 became known as Albert's *annus mirabilis* (Latin for "year of miracles"), just as 1665 had been the year of Newton. As subsequent experiments proved Albert's theories, he was embraced by Europe's scientific community, earning the admiration of such renowned scientists as Marie Curie and membership in such elite organizations as the Prussian Academy of Sciences.

Albert finally quit his job at the Swiss Patent Office in 1909, and over the next five years, the hopeful teacher no university had wanted a decade earlier was overwhelmed with offers from Europe's finest institutions. Albert bounced from one professorship to another, spending time at universities in Zurich and Prague, Czechoslovakia, before returning to his native land of Germany and a position at the University of Berlin in 1914. As Albert settled into his new surroundings, German troops invaded Belgium and France, starting World War I.

Louis de Broglie (pictured) won the 1929 Nobel Prize with his discoveries on the movements of atomic particles; his work was based on theories by Einstein and Max Planck.

A STAR IS BORN

German troops during World War I

Still, Albert's heart remained in mostly independent work. He felt more and more that his special theory of relativity did not go far enough; he believed relativity should apply not only to space and time, but to gravity as well. He focused his research during these years on a more encompassing proposal that would become his masterwork: the general theory of relativity.

Science was not the only thing on Albert's mind during his first years in Berlin. He was deeply troubled by the war raging throughout Europe, and in 1914, he took a public stand by signing the "Manifesto to Europeans," a public letter condemning Germany's aggression. This signaled the start of a lifelong campaign against war and a lasting rift with the German government.

Albert also faced a personal crisis: his deteriorating marriage. In 1914, Mileva and the boys went on a vacation in Switzerland, and the Einsteins never lived together as a family again. Albert and

EINSTEIN PUBLISHES A PAPER ON THE GENERAL THEORY OF RELATIVITY; IT BECOMES HIS MOST FAMOUS WORK. *Timeline* 1916

Mileva had both come to the realization that he preferred a more solitary life, unfettered by familial responsibilities. He later called the marriage "an undertaking in which I . . . failed rather disgracefully."

In 1916, Albert had his general theory of relativity published. He told skeptical physicists that proof of his theory—which explained that gravity is actually a curvature in space-time—could be obtained during a solar eclipse by monitoring the "bending" of starlight as it passed the sun. When evidence proved the theory in 1919, Albert's life changed instantly and forever. The world, still recovering from World War I, was eager for good news, and it found such cause for celebration in Albert's revision of the rules of the universe, and in Albert himself. The public came to see the 40-year-old—whose wild hair and decidedly unfashionable clothes made him a cartoonist's dream—as the definitive scientist.

Throughout the early 1920s, as his celebrity status reached fanatical proportions, Albert went on speaking tours to every corner of the world. He often traveled with his second wife, Elsa—a widowed cousin whom he had wed in 1919—and arrived by train on a third-class ticket, his violin tucked under one arm. On one such trip to Japan, Albert received word that he had won the 1921 Nobel Prize in Physics, mainly for his 1905 discovery of the photoelectric effect. He gave the $35,000 in prize money to Mileva.

Albert used his lecture tours to speak not only on science, but also against mandatory military service and in support of Jewish causes. Anti-Semitism, or hatred toward

"The future will show, more and more, the worth of Einstein, and the university which is able to capture this young master is certain of gaining much honor from the operation."

JULES POINCARÉ
FRENCH MATHEMATICIAN

Timeline **1919**   BRITISH ASTRONOMERS OBTAIN PROOF FOR EINSTEIN'S RELATIVITY THEORY, MAKING HIM WORLD-FAMOUS.

As Einstein grew more and more famous for his scientific theories, he took refuge in solitary moments, and in simple pleasures like smoking a favorite pipe.

Jews, was increasing in Europe, and even though Albert was a Jew in name only, never having practiced his faith, he felt a kinship with Jews and offered lifelong support to such causes as Zionism. Although Albert did not worship the traditional Judeo-Christian God, he did believe in a higher power, often speaking of God or a supreme being he called *Der Alte* ("The Old One").

By the end of the 1920s, Albert knew that his days in Berlin were numbered. He had long been reviled by anti-Semitic groups in Germany, who labeled his theories "radical Jewish ideas" and even made death threats against him. Now, as Adolf Hitler and the Nazis rose to power, Albert could again hear the drumbeat of war and turned his eyes westward toward the United States.

Albert had visited America for the first time in 1921 and was surprised to find that he was an even bigger celebrity in the U.S. than he was in Europe. He was also impressed by the high standards of scientific research being done there. In the early 1930s, the newly created Institute for Advanced Study in Princeton, New Jersey, offered Albert a position. In 1932, he accepted and soon left Europe for good.

EINSTEIN VISITS THE UNITED STATES FOR THE FIRST TIME TO LECTURE AND PROMOTE ZIONISM. *Timeline* 1921

As Hitler (pictured, right, with a member of the Hitler Youth) and the Nazis grew in number and spirit in Germany, Einstein left his home continent behind.

THE DAY THE WORLD CHANGED

BY THE TIME ALBERT LEFT HIS NATIVE LAND FOR AMER-
ICA, HE WAS NO LONGER SIMPLY A WELL-KNOWN PHYSI-
CIST—HE WAS A WORLD HERO AND CULTURAL ICON. THIS
TRANSFORMATION HAD OCCURRED LARGELY IN THE SPAN OF
A SINGLE DAY: NOVEMBER 6, 1919. THAT DAY, ENGLAND'S
TOP PHYSICISTS AND ASTRONOMERS—MEMBERS OF THE
ROYAL SOCIETY AND ROYAL ASTRONOMICAL SOCIETY—GATH-
ERED IN THE MAIN HALL OF LONDON'S BURLINGTON HOUSE.

English physicist J. J. Thomson

Royal Society president J. J. Thomson rose and addressed the gathering. Calling Albert's general theory of relativity "the greatest discovery in connection with gravitation since Newton," he went on to say that "our conceptions of the fabric of the universe must be fundamentally altered."

The events of this day were set in motion as early as 1907, when Albert came to the pivotal conclusion that gravity and accelera-tion are equal forces. Working from this premise, he published his finished general theory of relativity in 1916. The theory was incredibly complex, but its key concept was that massive objects such as stars and planets actually bend space and time, much as a heavy ball sitting on a mattress bends the surface. Objects with mass, including light particles, moving through space-time follow this curvature because it is the most direct path. The theory opened the doors to such mind-boggling possibilities as the existence of

EINSTEIN IS AWARDED THE NOBEL PRIZE IN PHYSICS FOR HIS WORK ON THE PHOTOELECTRIC EFFECT. *Timeline* **1922**

black holes and the expansion of the universe. General relativity could be proven during a solar eclipse, Albert said, by measuring how much a star's light curves.

In May 1919, a group of English astronomers traveled to two observatories—one on the island of Principe, off the west coast of Africa, the other in Brazil—where they would get an optimum view of a total solar eclipse. When the eclipse occurred on May 29, the astronomers made photographic plates, focusing in particular on a certain star near the edge of the sun. Albert waited anxiously for several months as the plates were developed and measured against previously captured images of the star.

When Albert had begun working on general relativity, a senior scientist had tried to dissuade him. "As an older man," he said, "I must advise you against it, for in the first place, you will not succeed. And even if you succeed, no one will believe you." But by 1919, the proof was in. At that November 6 gathering, astronomer Frank Dyson announced that analysis had proven Albert correct; the bending of light around the gravitational field of the sun had been almost exactly to the degree he had predicted.

On November 7, the *London Times* proclaimed a "Revolution in Science" with the headline: "New Theory of the Universe, Newtonian Ideas Overthrown." Papers throughout the world heralded the news, and Albert was declared the greatest genius on the planet. Almost overnight, he became a household name, his face the very image of brilliance. Albert was genuinely puzzled by the instant fame; he had

"He was almost wholly without sophistication.... There was always with him a wonderful purity at once childlike and profoundly stubborn."

ROBERT OPPENHEIMER
AMERICAN PHYSICIST

Timeline **1925**   EINSTEIN CAMPAIGNS WITH INDIAN CIVIL RIGHTS LEADER MAHATMA GANDHI FOR AN END TO MANDATORY MILITARY SERVICE.

Public interest in Einstein and his ideas soared with Einstein's new theory of relativity; in this 1930 photograph, reporters crowd him for an interview.

been publishing papers for well over a decade already, and now he was suddenly besieged by reporters and academics who hung on his every word. "I have no particular talent," he insisted. "I am merely inquisitive."

From that day forward, Albert would rarely be out of the news. Even people who would never meet him or attain anything more than a fleeting grasp of his contributions to science came to admire him. With his mild manners and childlike sense of wonder, Albert shattered the stereotype of the impersonable scientist who shut himself away from the world to pore endlessly over calculations. People learned of his bouts of absentmindedness—such as his tendency to misplace his keys or forget his suitcase on weekend visits—and came to see him as both an idol and a lovable dreamer.

Even though he generally found the media crush rather nonsensical, Albert tolerated the attention and inevitable misunderstanding of his ideas with great patience. Yet as the world embraced him, he longed to return to his work. At social events, he often seemed remote and distracted. He was a man of countless friends but few close ones, seeming to find more rewarding companionship in ideas. "Although I am a typical loner in daily life," he once said, "my consciousness of belonging to the invisible community of those who strive for truth, beauty, and justice has preserved me from feeling isolated."

In 1933, sculptor Jacob Epstein (right) created a bust honoring Einstein, whose popularity had soared with his permanent move to the U.S.

5 LIVING IN AMERICA

Einstein's home in Princeton, New Jersey

He lived with his wife, Elsa, and secretary, Helen Dukas. In 1939, his sister, Maja, would move in as well. For relaxation, he played the violin and took his sailboat out on Princeton's Lake Carnegie.

During his first years in the U.S., Albert watched sadly as Hitler turned Germany into a police state and began building Germany's army. Realizing that the rising Nazi war machine would not be stopped by principles, Albert astonished the world in 1933 by encouraging military action against Germany. "Organized power can be opposed only by organized power," he said. "Much as I regret this, there is no other way."

Even as Albert advocated taking up arms against his former homeland, the U.S. government cast a watchful eye on him. The American public revered Albert, but the Federal Bureau of Investigation, wary of a foreign scientist—particularly one known for his liberal views—living in America during a time of such international unrest, monitored him closely and ultimately compiled a 1,427-page file on him.

EINSTEIN WRITES TO U.S. PRESIDENT FRANKLIN ROOSEVELT, WARNING HIM OF THE NAZIS' WORK ON AN ATOMIC BOMB. *Timeline* 1939

In 1939, Germany invaded Poland, starting World War II. At about this time, Albert learned that Nazi scientists—basing their research largely on his E=mc² formula—had learned to split uranium atoms, the key to building a bomb that could unleash unfathomable destruction. Albert was staggered by the news; to the everlasting amazement of historians, the notion that the splitting of atoms could be used as a weapon apparently had never dawned on him.

In August 1939, Albert wrote a letter to U.S. President Franklin Roosevelt, warning him of Germany's efforts and suggesting that America consider creating its own atomic research program. Roosevelt took this advice to heart, creating the Manhattan Project. Germany was finally defeated in May 1945, but the war against Japan continued. Then, in August 1945, Albert learned with the rest of the world that the U.S. had succeeded in building a super-weapon when it annihilated the cities of Hiroshima and Nagasaki with atomic bombs. Albert would forever regret his role in the bomb's creation. "I could burn my fingers that I wrote that first letter to Roosevelt," he lamented.

Albert officially retired in 1945 but retained an office and continued to work on his unified field theory, an attempt to explain both gravity and electromagnetism in a single mathematical formula. Many scientists believed that such a formula was beyond reach; Albert agreed but embraced the challenge anyway. In 1948, he published his final, unsuccessful attempt at the theory.

> *"Many of us regard this as a tragedy, both for him, as he gropes his way in loneliness, and for us, who miss our leader and standard-bearer."*
>
> MAX BORN
> GERMAN PHYSICIST, ON ALBERT'S SEARCH FOR A UNIFIED FIELD THEORY

Timeline 1948   EINSTEIN PUBLISHES HIS LAST ATTEMPT AT A UNIFIED FIELD THEORY.

On August 9, 1945, a mushroom cloud towered 20,000 feet (6,100 m) high after the U.S. dropped an atomic bomb on Nagasaki to force Japan's surrender in World War II.

EINSTEIN IS OFFERED THE PRESIDENCY OF ISRAEL BUT TURNS THE POSITION DOWN.

The last decade of Albert's life was less about science than it was about a concern for humanity. In 1946, he became chairman of the Emergency Committee of Atomic Scientists, whose goal was world harmony and the abolition of atomic weapons. "My pacifism is an instinctive feeling," he explained. "A feeling that possesses me because the murder of men is disgusting."

By 1949, 70-year-old Albert's health was declining. Elsa had passed away in 1936, and his beloved sister had died in 1948. He kept in touch with his elder son, Hans Albert, an engineer and professor in California, but his younger son, Edward, was institutionalized with lifelong mental problems. Albert found companionship in these late years in the music of Mozart and the peacefulness of the Princeton campus. In 1952, Israel offered Albert its presidency. Although greatly flattered, he turned the offer down.

On April 16, 1955, an artery burst in Albert's abdomen. Doctors thought there was a slim chance that surgery could save him, but Albert declined, asking instead for his glasses and some paper so he could continue working. In the early morning hours of April 18, he mumbled his final words in German and died, concluding a life that was a testament to the incredible power of the human heart and mind. "Imagination is more important than knowledge," he once said. "Knowledge is limited. Imagination encircles the world."

ON APRIL 18, AT THE AGE OF 76, EINSTEIN DIES IN A PRINCETON HOSPITAL.   *Timeline* **1955**

This photograph shows a still-vivacious Einstein on the day before his 75th birthday; a burst artery ended his storied life approximately one year later.

IN HIS

WORDS

ORIGINALLY PUBLISHED IN 1934, THE FOLLOWING

EXCERPT WAS TAKEN FROM A COLLECTION OF ESSAYS

WRITTEN BY ALBERT EINSTEIN. HE TOUCHES ON A NUMBER

OF TOPICS RANGING FROM PACIFISM AND POLITICS TO HIS

THOUGHTS ON RELIGION AND THE MYSTERY OF GOD. THIS

ESSAY OFFERS A THOUGHTFUL AND EMOTIONAL GLIMPSE

INTO ANOTHER DIMENSION OF EINSTEIN, A MAN KNOWN

MOSTLY FOR HIS WORK AS A SCIENTIST WHO FOREVER

CHANGED THE WAY WE THINK ABOUT THE UNIVERSE.

THE MEANING OF LIFE *What is the meaning of human life, or of organic life altogether? To answer this question at all implies a religion. Is there any sense then, you ask, in putting it? I answer, the man who regards his own life and that of his fellow creatures as meaningless is not merely unfortunate but almost disqualified for life.*

THE WORLD AS I SEE IT *How extraordinary is the situation of us mortals! Each of us is here for a brief sojourn; for what purpose he knows not, though he sometimes thinks he senses it. But without going deeper than our daily life, it is plain that we exist for our fellow men—in the first place for those upon whose smiles and welfare all our happiness depends, and next for all those unknown to us personally but to whose destinies we are bound by the tie of sympathy. A hundred times every day I remind myself that my inner and outer life depend on the labors of other men, living and dead, and that I must exert myself in order to give in the same measure as I have received and am still receiving. I am strongly drawn to the simple life and am often oppressed by the feeling that I am engrossing an unnecessary amount of the labor of my fellow men. I regard class distinctions as contrary to* *justice and, in the last resort, based on force. I also consider that plain living is good for everybody, both physically and mentally.*

In human freedom in the philosophical sense, I am definitely a disbeliever. Everybody acts not only under external compulsion but also in accordance with inner necessity. Schopenhauer's saying, 'a man can do what he wants, but not want what he wants,' has been an inspiration to me since my youth up, and a continual consolation and unfailing well-spring of patience in the face of the hardships of life, my own and others. This feeling mercifully not only mitigates the sense of responsibility which so easily becomes paralyzing, but it also prevents us from taking ourselves and other people too seriously; it conduces to a view of life in which humor, above all, has its due place.

To enquire after the meaning or object of one's own existence or of creation generally has always seemed to me absurd from an objective point of view. And yet everybody has certain ideals which determine the direction of his endeavours and his judgments. In this sense, I have never looked upon ease and happiness as ends in themselves—on an ethical basis, I consider these the ideals of an inferior being. The ideals which have lighted me on my way and time after time given me new courage to face life cheerfully, have been Truth, Goodness, and Beauty. Without the sense of fellowship with men of like mind, of preoccupation with the objective, the eternally unattainable in the field of art and scientific research, life would have seemed to me empty. The ordinary objects of human endeavor—property, outward success, luxury—have always seemed to me contemptible.

My passionate sense of social justice and social responsibility has always contrasted oddly with my pronounced freedom from the need for direct contact with other human beings and human communities. I went my own way and have never belonged to my country, my home, my friends, or even my immediate family, with my whole heart; despite the existence of these ties, I have never lost an obstinate sense of detachment, of the need for solitude— a feeling which increases with the years. One becomes sharply conscious, without too much regret, of the limits of mutual understanding and sympathy between one's fellow creatures. One no doubt loses something in the way of cheerful bonhomie; on the other hand, one is largely independent of the opinions, habits, and judgments of one's fellows and avoids the temptation to take one's stand on such insecure foundations.

My political ideal is democratic. Let every man be respected as an individual and no man idolized. It is an irony of fate that I myself have been the recipient of excessive admiration and respect from my fellows, through no fault, and no merit of my own. The cause of this may well be the desire, unattainable for many, to understand the one or two ideas to which I have with my feeble powers attained through ceaseless struggle. I am quite aware that it is necessary for the achievement of any complex undertaking that one man should do the thinking and directing and in general bear the responsibility. But the led must not be compelled, they must be able to choose their leader. An autocratic system of coercion, in my opinion, soon degenerates. For force always attracts men of low morality, and I believe it to be an invariable rule that tyrants of genius are succeeded by scoundrels. For this reason, I have always been passionately opposed to systems such as we see in Italy and Russia today. The thing that has brought discredit upon the prevailing form of democracy in Europe today is not to be laid to the door of the democratic idea as such, but to lack of stability on the part of the heads of governments and to the impersonal character of the electoral system. I believe that in this respect the United States of America have found the right way. They have a President who is elected for a sufficiently long period and has sufficient powers to be really responsible. On the other hand, what I value in the German political system is the more extensive provision that it makes for the individual in case of illness or need. The really valuable thing in the pageant of human life seems to me not the political state, but the creative, sentient individual, the personality; it alone creates the noble and the sublime, while the herd as such remains dull in thought and dull in feeling.

This topic brings me to that worst outcrop of the herd nature, the military system, which I abhor. That a man can take pleasure in marching in fours to the strains of a band is enough to make me despise him. He has only been given his big brain by mistake; a backbone was all he needed. This plague-spot of civilization ought to be abolished with all possible speed. Heroism by order, senseless violence, and all the pestilent nonsense that goes by the name of patriotism—how I hate them! War seems to me a mean, contemptible thing: I would rather be hacked in pieces than take part in such an abominable business. And yet so high, in spite of everything, is my opinion of the human race that I believe this bogey would have disappeared long ago, had the sound sense of the nations not been systematically corrupted by commercial and political interests acting through the schools and the Press.

The fairest thing we can experience is the mysterious. It is the fundamental emotion which stands at the cradle of true art and true science. He who knows it not, and can no longer wonder, no longer feel amazement, is as good as dead, a snuffed-out candle. It was the experience of mystery—even if mixed with fear—that engendered religion. A knowledge of the existence of something we cannot penetrate, our perceptions of the profoundest reason and the most radiant beauty, which our minds seem to reach only in their most elementary forms—it is this knowledge and this emotion that constitute the truly religious attitude; in this sense, and in this alone, I am a deeply religious man. I cannot con-

ceive of a God who rewards and punishes his creatures, or has a will of the type of which we are conscious in ourselves. That an individual should survive his physical death is also beyond my comprehension, nor do I wish it otherwise; such notions are for the fears or absurd egoism of feeble souls. Enough for me are the mystery of the eternity of life and the inkling of the marvelous structure of reality, together with the single-hearted endeavor to comprehend a portion, be it ever so tiny, of the Reason that manifests itself in nature.

ADOLF HITLER The leader of the Nazi party; he became dictator of Germany in 1933 and led the country into World War II in an attempt to dominate Europe.

ATOMS The tiny parts that make up all forms of matter; atoms are made up of even smaller particles called protons, neutrons, and electrons.

BLACK HOLES Collapsed stars that have become so dense that not even light can escape their field of gravity; the first potential black hole was discovered in 1971.

ELECTROMAGNETISM A branch of physics that deals with the close relationship between electricity and magnetism; electricity can produce magnetism and vice versa.

FEDERAL BUREAU OF INVESTIGATION (FBI) A United States intelligence bureau that investigates an array of law violations that include spying and sabotage.

ISAAC NEWTON An English mathematician and physicist who, in the mid-1660s, laid the foundation for modern science through his discoveries on gravity, motion, and light.

ISRAEL A Jewish nation created in the Middle East in 1948; it was born out of the Zionist movement and prompted in part by atrocities against Jews in World War II.

MANHATTAN PROJECT America's top-secret atomic weapons program of the 1940s; it was headquartered at a desert base under the direction of physicist Robert Oppenheimer.

MARIE CURIE   A French chemist known for her work on radio-activity; she was among the first great female scientists and was twice awarded the Nobel Prize.

NAZIS   Members of the National Socialist German Workers' Party, a political party characterized by its racist views, strong national pride, and military aggression.

NOBEL PRIZE   A prestigious annual award that honors great achievements in physics, chemistry, medicine, literature, and the promotion of peace.

PACIFISM   The opposition to war or violence as a means of settling disputes; also the refusal to take part in military activity because of one's beliefs.

PHYSICS   The field of science that deals with matter, energy, force, and motion.

PYTHAGOREAN THEOREM   A famous mathematical puzzle—created by the ancient Greek philosopher Pythagoras—concerning the sides of a right triangle.

ZIONISM   An international movement whose main goal was the creation of a Jewish homeland (and from 1948 on, the support of the nation of Israel).